The World According to
Oprah

Other Books by Ken Lawrence

The World According to Michael Moore
The World According to Trump
The World According to Bill O'Reilly

The World According to Oprah

An Unauthorized Portrait in Her Own Words

KEN LAWRENCE

**Andrews McMeel
Publishing**

Kansas City

05 06 07 08 09 FFG 10 9 8 7 6 5 4 3 2 1

ISBN-13: 978-0-7407-5480-7
ISBN-10: 0-7407-5480-7

Library of Congress Cataloging-in-Publication Data
Lawrence, Ken.
   The world according to Oprah : an unauthorized portrait in her own words / Ken Lawrence.
      p. cm.
   ISBN: 0-7407-5480-7
   1. Winfrey, Oprah—Quotations. I. Title.

PN1992.4.W56A25 2005
791.4502'8'092—dc22

                                        2005045790

Design by Kelly & Company, Lee's Summit, Missouri

Contents

Introduction

OPRAH WINFREY is one of the most recognized people in the world. She has been on the covers of thousands of magazines and newspapers, has acted in hit movies, and has hosted the number-one-rated television talk show for almost twenty years. *The Oprah Winfrey Show* reaches more than thirty million viewers weekly in the United States and is broadcast to more than 110 countries.

This woman, who needs only one name to be identified by millions of people, is also one of the richest in the world, with an estimated worth of $1.3 billion, but this was not always the case.

Born in Kosciusko, Mississippi, on January 29, 1954, Oprah led an impoverished childhood—the farm had no indoor plumbing and the family used an outhouse. Oprah's parents were young and unmarried. Her father, Vernon Winfrey, was stationed at a local army base. Her mother, Vernita Lee, went to live in Milwaukee shortly after Oprah's birth to work as a maid, so Oprah spent her first few years with her grandmother, Hattie Mae Lee.

Precocious and rebellious, Oprah went to live with her mother in Milwaukee at the age of six. At thirteen, she was sent to a juvenile detention home but was turned away because of a lack of room. No longer able to handle her daughter, Vernita Lee sent Oprah to live with her father and stepmother in Nashville, where Vernon Winfrey raised his daughter with strict discipline and the notion that she could accomplish great things in her life with education and a belief in her abilities. He insisted that Oprah read books, and she often relied on them as an escape from her harsh life. "I don't know if my father has read a book in his entire life nor my stepmother. But they were educated enough to know that reading was important," she later told *Life* magazine.

At seventeen, Oprah had her first break. Nashville radio station WVOL hired her, and two years later she moved to WTVF-TV as a reporter and anchor. While anchoring the evening news there, she studied speech communication and performing arts at Tennessee State University.

In 1976, Oprah had an even bigger career opportunity, joining WJZ-TV in Baltimore as a coanchor of the *Six O'Clock News*. A few years later she became cohost of *People are Talking,* a local talk and interview show. Her popularity grew, especially among women, who identified with her because of her empathy and common touch.

In 1984, executives at Chicago's WLS-TV were looking for a personality to rescue *AM Chicago* from declining viewership. They took a chance on Oprah, and she didn't disappoint them. With Oprah's special gift for reaching an audience, the show not only became the most popular talk show in Chicago—eclipsing *Donahue*—but was expanded to one hour. It became *The Oprah Winfrey Show.*

In September 1986, *The Oprah Winfrey Show* went into national syndication and quickly became the country's most popular talk show. The following year, the show received three Daytime Emmy Awards. More awards followed, including the coveted Broadcaster of the Year Award from the International Radio and Television Society.

Oprah didn't confine herself to TV. In 1985, she began her acting career, playing Sofia in *The Color Purple,* Steven Spielberg's adaptation of Alice Walker's novel. Again, she earned accolades, including Best Supporting Actress Oscar and Golden Globe nominations. Her later film accomplishments include the production of the film *Beloved,* based on the Pulitzer Prize–winning novel by Toni Morrison, and performances in the made-for-TV movies *The Women of Brewster Place* in 1989, *There are no Children Here* in 1993, and *Before Women Had Wings* in 1997.

In 1988, Oprah established Harpo Studios, making her only the third woman in American entertainment—Mary Pickford and Lucille Ball were the first two—to own her own production facilities. With this move, she gained control of her financial and business future.

With her fortunes rising, Oprah founded the Oprah Winfrey Foundation in 1987 to support education for children, women, and families throughout the world. Ten years later, she established Oprah's Angel Network, a public charity that has raised nearly $20 million to help establish scholarships and support women's shelters and youth centers.

She was instrumental in the passage of the National Child Protection Act, which, partly due to her high-profile Congressional testimony and program of public awareness, was signed by President Bill Clinton in 1993. Nicknamed "the Oprah Bill," it protects children from abuse by establishing a national database of convicted child molesters.

Building on her reputation and name recognition, Oprah launched *O, The Oprah Magazine* in April 2000, describing it as "a different way for people to be informed and inspired." The magazine boasts a circulation of more than two million readers each month and has an international edition based in South Africa. Proceeds from the South African edition go toward scholarships and other causes—especially AIDS treatment and prevention—in that nation.

One of Oprah's greatest accomplishments has been the establishment of Oprah's Book Club, a feature on her TV show that highlights both contemporary and classic books. Because of Oprah's influence with audiences, books mentioned on the Book Club segments become instant best sellers and publishers are obliged to print tens of thousands of additional copies to meet demand.

Oprah extended her television reach in 1998 through the cofounding of Oxygen Media, which operates a twenty-four-hour cable network for women that reaches more than fifty-three million U.S. homes. In addition, in 2002, Oprah launched *Oprah After the Show,* which is taped immediately after her regular show and airs on the Oxygen network. It is unscripted, and, in Oprah's words, "allows us to let our hair down a little and just chat."

How this poor farm girl from Mississippi made her way from poverty and prejudice to one of the most loved, admired, and powerful people in the world is an inspiring story. Here, in her own empowering words, are the ideas and beliefs that make Oprah who she is today.

On Reading and
Oprah's Book Club

Reading books is the single greatest pleasure I have.

—*Entertainment Weekly*
OCTOBER 25, 1996

I don't know if my father has read a book in his entire life nor my stepmother. But they were educated enough to know that reading was important.

—*Life*
SEPTEMBER 1997

It has become harder and harder to find books on a monthly basis that I feel absolutely compelled to share. I will continue featuring books on *The Oprah Winfrey Show* when I feel they merit my heartfelt recommendation.

—From a written statement cited
by the *San Francisco Chronicle*
APRIL 6, 2002

*T*he reason I love books
is because they teach us
something about ourselves.

—*Chemist & Druggist*
JANUARY 15, 2000

*J*ohn Steinbeck [author of
East of Eden, whose book was
chosen to revive Oprah's Book
Club], wherever he is in the
spirit world, is very happy today.

—*Ottawa Citizen*
JUNE 29, 2003

*O*nce Maya Angelou had a party. It was a party for Toni [Morrison] after she received the Nobel Prize, and I went to it. I was surrounded by authors, and I felt like I was eleven years old. I felt like I could not even speak. At one point, somebody said, "Oh, I'd like some more coffee," and I got up to get it. Maya said, "Sit down," and I went, "No, I'll get it. It'd be a treat."

—*Guardian* (Manchester, England)
JANUARY 4, 2000

*S*o I think the possibilities of what could have happened to me versus what did happen to me are all based on a number of things, but certainly the ability to read and know that there was another world beyond sitting on that porch, beyond the outhouses. Pretty extraordinary when you think about it.

—*The Tavis Smiley Show*
OCTOBER 1, 2002

On Life
in America

*W*e are moving toward a nation that understands that we are one nation of many people of diverse backgrounds, but that we all share the same goals, the same interests. We are more alike than we are different— whether your grandfather came here on a boat or whether he came here on a boat not of his own will. It's important for people to come here to under- stand what has happened.

—*Cincinnati Post*
AUGUST 23, 2004

*A*mericans are a fearful people. We're all afraid to talk about what happened to us when we were ten years old, let alone what happened one hundred years ago. But the answer to that fear isn't to hide. It's to face the past. What I'm trying to tell people every day is to open the door and let the past in. You won't be swallowed by the past, you will be healed by the light that pours in.

—*Plain Dealer* (Cleveland, Ohio)
OCTOBER 11, 1998

*I*s America ready to heal
[the legacy of slavery]? We don't
know. I get asked that question
a lot and I say [that] some
people are—many people
are, and probably equally as
many are not.

—*Baltimore Sun*
OCTOBER 11, 1998

*I*t really doesn't matter where you live, but how you live. You find people in the projects who have as much desire for fulfillment and enrichment—to be somebody—as anywhere in the world.

—*Jet*
NOVEMBER 29, 1993

*I*f you live in the projects, [ABC's TV movie *There Are No Children Here*] is a story you already know too well, but I think the rest of America will be surprised to see how devastating life can be there.

—*Chicago Sun-Times*
NOVEMBER 28, 1993

On Television
and Her Show

*W*hen Donahue started, people thought women were only interested in manicure tips and how to stuff cabbage, and Donahue showed they were interested in their lives and in other interests in their lives. And I thank him for paving the way.

—*Los Angeles Times*
JULY 1, 1987

*W*hen we first started, if someone cried onscreen then it was an event. Now I have to get people to stop crying. I say to them, you can hold on, don't break down. You see, there are so many chat shows in America today, viewers have become accustomed to them. Now they are more willing to be freer in their thinking and talking in front of a camera.

—*Guardian* (Manchester, England)
OCTOBER 18, 1989

*T*his [show with neo-Nazi skinheads] has been somewhat out of control. I've never seen such or felt such evilness or hatred in all my life.

—*Los Angeles Times*
FEBRUARY 5, 1988

*M*y show is really a ministry, a ministry that doesn't ask for money. I can't tell you how many lives we've changed— or inspired to change.

—*Los Angeles Times*
DECEMBER 20, 1987

I do not pay for interviews,
no matter what the payment
is called.

—Eonline.com
SEPTEMBER 30, 1998

I'm the first black woman in
this country to have a nationally
syndicated talk show and it seems
to me like that would be worth
celebrating.

—*Washington Post*
JULY 19, 1987

I live my life and I do this show to try to raise people's consciousness, to give people a sense of hope in their lives. So when people write or say negative things like that about me it really upsets me, because it means they don't understand me or what my show is about. They've missed it. But I'm convinced that if people who believe that really got to know me, they wouldn't think I was that kind of person.

—*Saturday Evening Post*
JULY 1987

I dream about finding a new way of doing television that elevates us all. I really am tired of the crud. My goal for myself is to reach the highest level of humanity that is possible to me. Then, when I'm done, when I quit the planet, I want to be able to say, "Boy, I did that, didn't I? Yes, I did!"

—*Redbook*
MAY 1997

I remember [nervously] sitting in my chair [when interviewing John F. Kennedy Jr.] and telling myself, "Just keep breathing."

—*Entertainment Weekly*
DECEMBER 27, 1996

*W*e're going to kick off our shoes [in *Oprah After the Show*], take questions from the audience, and see where the conversation takes us.

—*Toronto Star*
JUNE 12, 2002

*O*riginally our goal was to uplift, enlighten, encourage, and entertain through the medium of television. Now, our mission … is to use television to transform people's lives, to make viewers see themselves differently, and to bring happiness and a sense of fulfillment into every home.

—*Chicago Sun-Times*
OCTOBER 29, 2000

*T*he general manager at my station said to me, "You know you can't beat *Donahue,* so just go on the air and be yourself."

—*Essence*
OCTOBER 2003

*I*t's fulfilling being able to do this kind of television, and I believe continuing to have a voice and a platform to speak to the world is still the right thing to do.

—*Guardian* (Charlottetown, Prince Edward Island, Canada)
JUNE 11, 2003

*A*nd then I did [*Beloved*] and I realized that having a voice and being able to speak to the world in people's homes is a real privilege. It's not just a television show. Good God almighty, you're sitting in somebody's house ... when they're naked ... and they know you!

—*Sun-Sentinel*
(Fort Lauderdale, Florida)
OCTOBER 14, 1998

*A*t that time, [when I was filming *Beloved*], I was thinking of not going on with the television show. I had thought that I'll get into this movie and I'll make more movies and it'll just be great—I won't have to do two hundred shows a year. But ... how can you come from no voice—from a legacy of "Your thoughts don't even belong to you"—to now being able to speak to the world. I decided I couldn't give it up.

—*Los Angeles Times*
SEPTEMBER 13, 1998

I want to use television not only to entertain but to help people lead better lives.

—*Success*
MAY 1998

I've been successful all these years because I do my show with the people in mind, not for the corporations or their money.

—*People*
FEBRUARY 16, 1998

*T*his is not a news magazine.
I'm a talk show where the
expression of opinions are
encouraged. This is the United
States, and we are allowed to
do that in the United States.

—*Chicago Tribune*
FEBRUARY 8, 1998

I love that lightbulb moment
when you can actually see
[the audience] get it, to figure
out the point.

—*Chicago Tribune*
NOVEMBER 10, 1997

I think we did a really good job of pulling ourselves away from the "trash pack" last year.

—*Baltimore Sun*
SEPTEMBER 6, 1995

*T*his season has proved that there are endless possibilities to entertain and empower people's lives through television. As long as we carry out that mission and the show remains fulfilling to me, I will continue to do *The Oprah Winfrey Show.*

—*Jet*
APRIL 4, 1994

I am every one of [my audience], and they are me. That's why we get along so well. I'm vulnerable like them and people say "Poor thing. She has big hips, too." It crosses racial barriers.

—*Guardian* (Manchester, England)
APRIL 25, 1991

*T*he thought of taking
the show to its twenty-fifth
anniversary is both exhilarating
and challenging.

> —*Akron Beacon Journal* (Ohio)
> AUGUST 9, 2004

I would not be able to do
my show if it were not for Phil
Donahue, who thought women
were interested in subjects
beyond putting on their mascara.

> —*Independent* (London)
> SEPTEMBER 18, 1993

*U*nless you are going to kill people on the air, and not just hit them on the head with chairs, and unless you are going to have sexual intercourse—and not just, as I saw the other day, a guy pulling down his pants . . . then there comes a point when you have oversaturated yourself.

—*Philadelphia Inquirer*
FEBRUARY 10, 1999

On Her Struggle with Weight

*E*very day for the rest of my life is going to be a struggle not to succumb once more to the old buffet table. I am by no means through.

—*New York Times*
NOVEMBER 24, 1988

*G*od blessed me with a great structure, just a little too much of it. And if you don't believe me, ask the folks at Anne Klein.

—*People*
FEBRUARY 2, 1987

I made a bet with Joan Rivers
on national TV that I'd lose
weight, so I was on a health
farm when Reuben, the casting
agent, called me and told me
I had the role [of Sofia in
The Color Purple]. "If you lose
a pound you'll lose this part,"
he screamed. So I got my
behind to Dairy Queen.

—*Toronto Star*
SEPTEMBER 14, 1988

*T*here was a pizza booth, a corn dog booth, and my favorite at the time, a giant chocolate chip cookie stall. You could order an eighteen-inch chocolate chip cookie with or without macadamia nuts. I loved macadamia nuts. I always ordered the kind with them. On weekends, I'd stroll the mall, going from stall to stall. Sometimes I'd order something from every booth. I didn't realize at the time that by overeating I was trying to fill something deeper, something unconscious.

—*Buffalo News* (New York)
FEBRUARY 9, 1997

*F*or two years before I met [my personal trainer] Bob, I ate only low-fat meals and snacks. Not only did I not lose weight, I gained. Partly because I never learned when to stop eating. I was a compulsive emotional eater.

—*Sun-Sentinel*
(Fort Lauderdale, Florida)
OCTOBER 9, 1996

$\mathcal{L}$osing weight on a liquid diet and exercise program] has been the most difficult thing I have ever done in my life. Not one single thing I have ever done has measured up to this kind of accomplishment.

—*Entertainment Weekly*
NOVEMBER 17, 2000

*W*e were the largest human beings on the entire island of St. Tropez. You sit by these girls and you feel like an elephant, you feel like a cow, you feel like, "I don't even work out."

> —*Orange County Register*
> (California)
> SEPTEMBER 2, 1995

*A*fter every show women tell me, "You look so good. How do you keep it off?" Then I say, "Well, I work out this hard." And they're not willing to get up at 5 a.m. It's not in the recipes. There's no secret recipe.

—*Detroit Free Press*
APRIL 28, 1995

I've been dieting since 1977, and the reason I failed is that diets don't work. I tell people, if you're underweight, go on a diet and you'll gain everything you lost plus more. Now I'm trying to find a way to live in a world with food without being controlled by it, without being a compulsive eater. That's why I say I will never diet again.

—*People*
JANUARY 14, 1991

On Her

Acting Career

*A*nd the most taxing thing, which I hadn't figured, is the emotional toll that acting plays on your body and spirit—the exhaustion factor.

—*Los Angeles Times*
MAY 1, 1990

*I*n a society that is so media controlled, doing good film is one of the best ways to raise consciousness. You present the story, and then you let people choose to change the way things are or not. I want to make a difference. I want that on my tombstone.

—*New York Times*
MARCH 12, 1989

I will never do another film about slavery. I won't try to touch race again in this form, because people just aren't ready to hear it.

—*Guardian* (Manchester, England)
FEBRUARY 13, 1999

*A*fter I read the book. I felt that *Beloved* was part of the reason I was born, to tell the story on screen.

—*Saturday Evening Post*
JANUARY 1999

*A*bout a week before filming [*Beloved*] started, I went through a slavery reenactment. I was blindfolded and put on a trek in Maryland that used to be part of the Underground Railroad, where slaves walked trying to reach freedom. I needed to know what it felt like to be out in the wilderness, barefoot and lost. People slept in trees in the daytime and ran at night. I wanted to know the feeling of being scared, with snakes around, wondering where you were going to sleep. What do you eat? Where do you put your baby?

—*Good Housekeeping*
DECEMBER 1998

*T*he experience of doing *Beloved* has been transforming. It has put me in the knowing place of where I come from. I come out of it more determined than ever to soar because that is my foundation.

—*Jet*
OCTOBER 19, 1998

I had some self-doubt as the years passed about whether or not I would actually be able to pull [*Beloved*] off. I told every director that I met with that if I can't pull it off, I'd be glad to give it to somebody else. None of them believed me. It was more important to me that the story get told, and I felt that if I couldn't do it, I wanted to find the best person who could.

—*Dallas Morning News*
OCTOBER 11, 1998

*D*oing the television show is easy. I just go on and be Oprah. Acting is something else, and acting in a piece like this one— well, we were all emotionally devastated by it. I tried to strip all of Oprah away to be Sethe [in *Beloved*], but it was so hard. Some days, I would just cry and cry for Sethe, and for my grandma and for myself, you know? Then I would have to go be strong Sethe again.

—*Detroit Free Press*
OCTOBER 11, 1998

*P*eople who come out say they're staggered by this movie [*Beloved*], they're numb, dumb-founded, overwhelmed, devastated. I think that's a good thing.

—*Hartford Courant* (Connecticut)
OCTOBER 11, 1998

*T*he challenge was to feel this story instead of just showing it. I wanted a film that you would come away from not having just seen it, but experienced it.

—*Kansas City Star*
OCTOBER 11, 1998

I told my people that they shouldn't call me [while I was acting] unless the John Hancock Building, which is next door to our building, fell over and landed on our building. If it fell over and missed our building, I didn't want to hear from them.

—*Star Tribune*
(Minneapolis, Minnesota)
OCTOBER 11, 1998

I bought the [Harpo Films] studio with the idea that I'd finish the talk show, go to the next [sound] stage and put on the *Brewster Place* character's clothes. . . . Hah! Thought I could work twenty-hour days on a consistent basis. Hah!

—*Philadelphia Inquirer*
OCTOBER 11, 1998

On Family

I hated [my father] and my stepmother, Zelma, as I was growing up because of all the restrictions they put on me, but I adore them today. My father is a kind and generous man—the kind of man I want to marry.

—*Toronto Star*
JANUARY 10, 1987

I cannot even imagine what it would be like to lose a child or a family member. I wonder: Will [victims of the Oklahoma federal building bombing] ever sleep again?

—*USA Today*
APRIL 26, 1995

*M*y father turned my life around by insisting I could be more than I was.

—*Guardian* (Manchester, England)
JULY 20, 1993

*M*y grandmother taught me
that prayer is the most valuable
tool you could have. And always
pray on your knees because
one day you won't be able to
bend down.

—*San Jose Mercury News*
(California)
MAY 5, 2004

On Being Famous

*W*hen you get to the point where you become so-called famous you really need to be able to surround yourself with people who can tell you the truth.

—*Fort Worth Star-Telegram*
MAY 6, 2004

*E*verybody is valuable, and all people should be treated with a sense of dignity and grace. To rush past all those people [after being hustled into a limousine by bodyguards] just wasn't right. I can still hear that "boo," and it hurts.

—*Orange County Register*
(California)
NOVEMBER 3, 1989

I'll tell you what being famous
has done. I got up this morning
and jogged six miles. Then
I really wanted pancakes for
breakfast. With homemade
applesauce. Well, Tony Curtis
is sitting at the next table and
I know he's not going to tell, but
maybe the chef will. So I had my
boyfriend Stedman order them
and we shared. That's what
being famous does to you.

—*Toronto Star*
MARCH 18, 1989

$\mathcal{T}$V's Peabody Award is] certainly not anything I ever expected to win myself. This is a great honor because of everyone who has won it in the past and the sense of prestige attached to it.

—*Chicago Sun-Times*
APRIL 11, 1996

*T*his past September I received [the Bob Hope] Humanitarian Award. I got up from the stage and I was standing there and everybody then stood up. I got a standing ovation at the Emmys. And just for a moment, I mean, it was like a flicker. I went, "Oh, this is what fame is." And just as I was walking off the stage with Tom Hanks, I turned and I looked back just to think, did that really happen? Did that really happen? Yeah, that must be what being famous is.

—*Good Morning America*
JULY 1, 2003

I have a real global vision for what I can do with this so-called fame.

—U.S. Newswire, citing
The Tavis Smiley Show
SEPTEMBER 27, 2002

*U*nderstand that when you are a "celebrity," people treat you differently, period, regardless of what color you are.

—*Irish Times*
MARCH 11, 1995

On Charity
and Giving

I'm not trying to be some
evangelist. The intention [of
asking people to give spare
change to fund scholarships]
is to try and get people to
feel some illumination.

—*People Special*
MARCH 15, 1999

*Y*ou can't save the world, but
you can save [one youngster
like] Troy.

—*People*
NOVEMBER 29, 1993

I want the [scholarship money to Morehouse College] to go to young, African American men. . . . Nothing has been more rewarding to me than to know that my life has touched another life. I think that is what God would have intended for me and for all of us.

—*Jet*
DECEMBER 8, 1997

𝒴ou can reach out. You can be a princess, a queen in your own life by taking what you have and extending it to other people. So I've asked people to tell me about many miracles that they've created in other people's lives, and it's really the most rewarding season I've ever had on television thus far.

—*Jet*
NOVEMBER 24, 1997

*I*t is my intention to take people out [of inadequate Chicago public housing], to change their lives. But more importantly than changing their lives, I want to change the way they think about their lives. I want to destroy the welfare mentality.

—*Chicago Tribune*
SEPTEMBER 14, 1994

*M*y favorite part [of the show that gave away cars] was when I announced the first ten who really, really needed cars because they had such old clinkers, and they were so excited. I wasn't so sure that was gonna happen. Sometimes people just don't give you any kind of reaction. When I saw their reaction and how overwhelmed they were, I thought, "Oh, I got 'em!"

—*People*
SEPTEMBER 27, 2004

*T*he car giveaway] was first proposed to me by one of the producers as a favorite things idea, and I said, "You know, that's not going to work for me because I think a car is a nice gift if you don't need it, if you already have one, but it really can change your life if you really need one." So, I said, "To me, it would be more important to have an entire audience filled with people who could really get some value out of having a new car."

—*Good Morning America*
SEPTEMBER 14, 2004

*M*y dream was—when I first started making money—to pass it on and I wanted to put 100 men through Morehouse [College]. Right now we're at 250 and I want to make it a thousand.... Before I leave here tonight Saturday I want to leave another $5 million check with Dr. Massey.

—*Los Angeles Sentinel*
MARCH 3, 2004

You know, the best Christmas I ever remember having was when I was twelve years old and living with my mother in Milwaukee, and my mother was on welfare, taking care of me and another half-sister and brother. And she'd come to me as the oldest and said, "We won't be having Christmas this year...." We'd all gone to bed and I remember the doorbell ringing and three nuns showed up at our house. And they had

bought food, a turkey. And they
bought toys for my half-sister
and half-brother and for myself.…
And that, in my memory, was
the strongest feeling I'd ever had
of somebody lifting me up—
just, just their kindness really
made me feel so much better
about myself, that I never forgot
it. So, I thought, how could I do
that for somebody else? And
I thought, Africa.

—*Good Morning America*
DECEMBER 17, 2003

*Y*ou can [give charity] right
here in Waukesha County.
You don't have to go to Africa
to extend yourself.

—Associated Press
OCTOBER 27, 2003

I've had some proud moments in television, and this is one of them. It's way up there at the top. [*Scared Silent*] is what television should do. . . . I know this special is going to make a major, major difference for a great number of people.

—*Chicago Sun-Times*
AUGUST 30, 1992

*M*y idea [to give profits from the South African edition of *O, The Oprah Magazine* to charity] is to give hope, because where there is no hope, there is no vision, and where there is no vision, people will perish.

—*Africa News*
DECEMBER 5, 2002

On Children

I believe that one of a nation's most important resources is its young people, and the key that allows young people to create a better world and a brighter future is education.

—*Black Issues in Higher Education*
JUNE 6, 2002

I'm always looking for ways
that I can use myself and use
my life, use my money, use my
time, use my energy. What I'm
interested in doing now is
creating a lasting impact. . . .
My efforts [are] going into
schools because education
is freedom.

—*Larry King Live*
DECEMBER 9, 2003

*W*hat happens to a generation of children left to fend for themselves? Unless someone does something now the orphans will change the face of [South Africa] and the continent.

—Associated Press
DECEMBER 21, 2002

*O*ne of the reasons I am here is to humanize this pandemic. I want people to see the real hearts and souls of South African orphans infected with HIV/AIDS.

—Agence France-Presse
DECEMBER 7, 2002

*B*alance? That's why I don't have children. People in my audience are always saying they want me to have kids, and I always tell them I have to start this evening because that clock is about run out.

—*Fortune*
OCTOBER 12, 1998

For right now I feel I can
make greater contributions
to the world's children. What
[parenthood] takes is one-on-
one time, which I don't have.

—*Jet*
SEPTEMBER 19, 1994

*T*here are thousands more
who will no longer remain silent
[after watching the film *Scared
Silent*]. It has empowered children,
and adult children everywhere
so they know they do not have
to stand alone. It's time to stop
the pain and suffering of children,
and make the world a safer
place for all of us.

—*Children Today*
MARCH 1992

*W*hen I was abused, I blamed myself. I blamed myself for most of my adult life. You lose your childhood once you've been abused.

—*Orlando Sentinel* (Florida)
NOVEMBER 13, 1991

*M*y life was dramatically changed. These children [in Africa with AIDS] are just like yours. They want to feel safe, they want to laugh and play, and they want to know that they matter.

—*Orange County Register*
(California)
JULY 8, 2004

On Jury Duty

*W*hen you see a mother
who has lost a son in this manner,
it's something I think you never
forget, and that is an impression
that will be with me forever.

—*Good Morning America*
AUGUST 19, 2004

$\mathcal{T}$he bigger story here for me is a man is dead, murdered, supposedly over $50, and that the real war is still going on in the inner-city streets every day. Young black men killing each other. [It was] one of the saddest, saddest experiences I've ever had.

—Reuters
AUGUST 18, 2004

*I*t's a huge reality check. There's a whole other world going on out there.... When your life intersects with others in this way, it is forever changed.

—Associated Press
AUGUST 18, 2004

I would not have me on a jury.

—United Press International
AUGUST 17, 2004

*Y*ou're not allowed to discuss anything to do with the trial until the whole thing is over, and so you get to know people really, really well because you're trying to talk about everything else.

—*Windsor Star* (Ontario)
AUGUST 28, 2004

*T*his is not good for the victim's family....This is not about Oprah Winfrey; the fact is a man has been murdered.

—*Moscow News* (Russia)
AUGUST 25, 2004

*T*he guilty verdict] was not an easy decision to make. All of us have taken to heart this decision.

—*Toronto Star*
AUGUST 20, 2004

I'm just hoping it doesn't take longer than a week, because I have shows to do.

—*National Post* (Toronto)
AUGUST 18, 2004

On O,
The Oprah Magazine

*L*ook, I know that to [the editors] the Oprah name is a brand. But for me, it is my life, it's the way I live my life, and everything I stand for.

—*Baltimore Sun*
APRIL 17, 2000

*T*his magazine provides a different way for people to be informed and inspired.

—*New York Times*
JULY 9, 1999

*I*t's the book I never wrote.

—*Philadelphia Inquirer*
APRIL 16, 2000

*T*here are many times in
my magazine when I have not
agreed with the editor, and we
just talk it out. Sometimes I let
it go. And there are other times
where I feel strongly enough
about it, and I say that absolutely
cannot happen. Because it's an
O on the magazine.

—*Time*
DECEMBER 15, 2003

On Prosperity
and Money

*I*n vision there is sharing.
In sharing there is growth.
In growth there is prosperity....
At the basis of prosperity is the
spiritual realization of who we
all are.

—Los Angeles Times
APRIL 21, 1987

*W*ith all this fame and money,
I have to do something more
than buy shoes.

—People
DECEMBER 28, 1987

*H*ey, Gayle [referring to her friend Gayle King], it's the Casual Corner all over again, only this time we're buying a Bentley!

—*People*
FEBRUARY 23, 1998

*A*lthough I'm grateful for the blessings of wealth, it hasn't changed who I am. My feet are still on the ground. I'm just wearing better shoes.

—*Times* (London)
JULY 16, 2004

*I*t turns out this was the
most expensive sandwich
I've ever had.

> —On investing in the Art Cafe and
> Bakery after a restaurant photo
> shoot for an issue of *O, The Oprah
> Magazine,* as reported in *Guelph
> Mercury* (Ontario)
> JULY 27, 2004

*Q*uestion: What would you
do with a million dollars?

Answer: I'd be a spending fool.

> —Interview segment with Oprah
> in the Miss Black America
> pageant in 1971, as quoted
> by *Philippine Daily Inquirer*
> DECEMBER 21, 2002

On Romance
and Relationships

*W*hat really matters is who you love and how you love.

—Speech at *Prayer for America* service at New York's Yankee Stadium for victims of 9/11, cited by CNN.com
SEPTEMBER 23, 2001

*M*y idea of heaven is a big baked potato and someone to share it with.

—*Evening Times* (Glasgow, Scotland)
NOVEMBER 27, 2003

David and Lisa is a timeless love story. It's a story I wanted to tell to a whole new generation. Like David, sometimes we can get consumed by fears and anxieties. So we play it safe. But when you really love somebody, you can take that risk. You're transformed. You're no longer the same person.

—*Baltimore Sun*
OCTOBER 31, 1998

*I*t does scare me a little bit, the whole idea of being married to somebody for the rest of your life. You don't want to wake up ten years from now and say, "My God, who is this I've married?" So it scares me a little bit, but I think it's the right thing to do.

—*Jet*
NOVEMBER 23, 1992

I have the right to *not* get married. I'm sorry I ever was such a bigmouth frog about the engagement [to Stedman Graham]. That is my biggest public regret.

—*Redbook*
AUGUST 1996

I went to Africa to create the best Christmas possible for kids who'd never had one. And the joy in that room was so thick you physically feel it. In that moment, it hit me. Now I see why I am not married. Now I see why I never had children. I am supposed to work with these children.

—United Press International
SEPTEMBER 27, 2003

I think Mr. Right is coming,
only he must be in India and
he's walking to get here.

—*Washington Post*
OCTOBER 21, 1986

T hank you, too, Stedman
for putting up with all the long
hours—it's our sixth anniversary!

—Upon accepting an Emmy,
cited by *Jet*
JULY 13, 1992

On Her
Spiritual Side

I am guided by a higher calling. It's not so much a voice as it is a feeling. If it doesn't feel right to me, I don't do it.

—*Time*
AUGUST 8, 1988

*Y*ou come from a power source and therefore you have great power. And the moment you recognize that power, you will recognize that power is God.

—*Orange County Register*
(California)
APRIL 21, 1987

I don't need to bring home other people's dysfunctions. I have my own dysfunctions.

—*Atlanta Journal-Constitution*
OCTOBER 30, 1995

I believe when you lose a loved one, you gain an angel whose name you know.

—*Business Week*
JANUARY 14, 2002

I didn't know what the future held for me [in moving from Baltimore to Chicago]. But I knew who held the future.

—*Baltimore Sun*
JULY 2, 2001

I just left everything there [upon selling several condos in Florida's Fisher Island]—dishes, napkin holders. I'm not attached to material things.

—*People*
JULY 2, 2001

I feel tremendously powerful because I do believe I have reached a point in life where my personality is aligned with what my soul came to do.
I believe you have to use your ego for a higher good.

—*Essence*
OCTOBER 2003

*T*he common denominator in the human experience is the need for validation. What I teach is you do matter. You matter because you were born.

—Seattle Times
JUNE 1, 2003

*A*ll that I am or will ever become is because of my spiritual foundation and my educational foundation. My life is a living testimony to what God can do with a human being.

—Associated Press
NOVEMBER 11, 2002

*Y*ou become what you believe.

—Associated Press
NOVEMBER 9, 2002

*W*e live in a world that
observes our external selves.
What's significant, however, is
finding a deeper meaning so
that your life has a better
balance and wholeness.

—*Irish Times*
AUGUST 5, 2000

$\mathcal{T}$o heck with the critics.
They're always going to be
there. You say "This is who I am"
and the rest of the world tells
you who you think you are.
I know intellectually, spiritually,
that you cannot proclaim
anything in your life without
having some force come up
and challenge it.

—*Sun-Sentinel*
(Fort Lauderdale, Forida)
SEPTEMBER 7, 1999

*S*pirit is not a religion; it's just about what is really great about yourself and remembering to live that way.

—*New York Times*
NOVEMBER 8, 1998

*N*ow I know what my people always knew, which is that you have to look inside yourself and find the spirit to say, "I am better than this." To me that is the ultimate fearlessness.

—*Ottawa Citizen*
OCTOBER 7, 1998

I learned that you have to be careful what you ask for, because when you get it, the form may not be exactly what you had in mind.

—*TV Guide*
JANUARY 7, 1995

W orking on a book] has been for me like ten years of therapy. I've learned so much about myself.

—*Hartford Courant* (Connecticut)
JUNE 1, 1993

I think everybody has to figure out a way—I think the real job of your life is figuring out what is the job of your life. What is your calling? And I think everybody is called here to earth to do something special. I think there's not a person born that doesn't have a gift to offer in some way. And so, your job is not just to do what your parents say, what your teachers say, what society says, but to figure out what your heart calling is and to be led by that.

—*Larry King Live*
DECEMBER 20, 2003

On Success

*R*eal success comes when you learn to act as if everything depends on you, and pray as if everything depends on God. God can dream a bigger dream for you than you can ever dream for yourself.

—*Atlanta Journal-Constitution*
MAY 17, 1999

I didn't have a plan for success, but twelve years ago, I said, "The future's so bright it burns my eyes." I've always had a very strong faith in God, that if I would try to align my will with the will of the creator, that I could not fail.

—*Guardian* (Manchester, England)
MAY 10, 1997

$\mathcal{T}$here were no role models
for me but Buckwheat, and
nobody wanted to be Buck-
wheat but Buckwheat. I stand
on solid rock because I come
from a great legacy of black
people. I was never taught
oppression.

—*Los Angeles Times*
OCTOBER 24, 1988

*W*hen I first saw Amblin [studio] three years ago during my audition for *The Color Purple,* I thought, "One day I want to own a place like this." It was a dream of mine ... but I did not know it would happen this fast.

—*Chicago Tribune*
SEPTEMBER 18, 1988

I was raised with an outhouse, no plumbing. Nobody had any clue that my life could be anything but working in some factory or a cotton field in Mississippi. Nobody—nobody.... I feel so strongly that my life is to be used as an example to show people what can be done.

—*Pittsburgh Post-Gazette*
MAY 19, 1997

*F*rom the time we are born,
we are empowered to take
control over our lives and do
with our lives what we will. Once
you realize that, victory is yours.

—*St. Petersburg Times* (Florida)
MARCH 13, 1987

*S*tep out, step up, and step
into the life you were meant to
live ... and step out of the box
of people's limitations for you.

—*Herald* (Glasgow, Scotland)
APRIL 17, 2001

*I*t appears I have everything,
but I have struggled with my
own self-value for many, many
years. And I am just now coming
to terms with it.

—*People*
DECEMBER 27, 1993

*W*omen try to do too much
instead of reaching out and
asking for support so they can
do what they do better. Always
do your best, because you never
know who's watching.

—Associated Press
JULY 26, 2004

*N*o dream is too wild, no surprise too impossible to pull off.

—*Calgary Sun* (Alberta)
SEPTEMBER 14, 2004

*L*uck is a matter of preparation. I am highly attuned to my divine self, . . . I always knew that I was born for greatness.

—*Independent* (London)
MARCH 13, 1990

*E*very day you get out there and do your best. I'm myself, and I hope it works.

—*Chicago Tribune*
JANUARY 31, 1985

*I*t has always been a dream of mine to teach.

—*Ottawa Citizen*
MAY 20, 1999

*A*t fifty you know a lot more than you did when you were twenty-five, so you can use all that stuff you didn't know to propel yourself forward. I feel like [turning fifty] is everything you were meant to be in your life.

—*People*
FEBRUARY 2, 2004

*W*hen it's me at a boardroom table surrounded by
fifteen white guys, I think of a
photo of Katharine Graham in
her book. It's a picture of her
sitting at that table, as head
of the *Washington Post,*
surrounded by all white guys.
[When I walk into the room,
I bring] with me Sojourner Truth
and Harriet Tubman and all the
women who never made it into
a boardroom. And I'm ready for
the meeting.

—*Inc.*
SEPTEMBER 2001

On Speaking Out

I will continue to use my voice. I believed from the beginning that [the beef industry lawsuit] was an attempt to muzzle my voice, and I come from a people who have struggled and died in order to have a voice in this country. And I refused to be muzzled.

—CNN.com
FEBRUARY 26, 1998

*I*t has just stopped me from eating another burger!

—After a guest told her that feeding ground-up animal parts to cattle could spread mad cow disease to humans, cited by *Pittsburgh Post-Gazette*
JUNE 19, 1997

*I*f I can't take a risk, nobody can. With fame, notoriety, credibility—if you can't have the courage to stand up and speak out for what you truly believe in, then it means nothing.

—*People*
DECEMBER 28, 1998

*F*ree speech not only lives, it rocks. I took it for granted, and I never will again.

—*Supermarket News*
MARCH 2, 1998

I felt it was important to be here to face this courtroom [in the beef industry lawsuit] and the jurors and to defend my name. It's the most painful thing I've ever experienced. In the end, all you have is your reputation.

—*St. Louis Post-Dispatch* (Missouri)
FEBRUARY 7, 1998

I intend to take a stand and do the kind of shows that are important to me and I believe that will be of importance to the rest of the country. Because I feel that in spite of my fame and wealth, that the core of me is like everybody else.

—*Boston Herald*
NOVEMBER 6, 1994

*I*believe we had right on our side from the beginning [in her court case involving the beef industry]. But you never know. Twelve people can see things twelve separate ways.

—*Chicago Tribune*
FEBRUARY 26, 1998

What Others Say About Oprah

*S*he goes out on the line and says to her viewers, "I love this book, here are the reasons why I love this book, and here's why I want you to read this book." That's the difference between her club and other clubs.

—Paul Bogaards, executive director
of publicity at Alfred A. Knopf,
quoted by the Associated Press
JUNE 14, 2003

You know, Oprah's show has caused me to lose some money between nine and ten in the morning. That's because I need my eyes to cut hair and to watch her. The haircuts keep me from getting the full significance of it sometimes.

—Vernon Winfrey, quoted
in the *Washington Post*
DECEMBER 14, 1986

She just wouldn't listen to
her mother. She needed some
discipline to make sure she got
a good start.

—Vernon Winfrey, quoted in *People*
DECEMBER 16, 1985

She really has it together. You
can tell in the way she moves.

—Longtime friend Gayle King,
quoted in *People*
MAY 12, 1997

*S*he's like the friend you always connect with, the one who catches you up on her life; you know, the one you confide in.

—Maryann Koehl, an airline worker from Palatine, Illinois, who sometimes tapes the show when she is on the job, quoted in the *Los Angeles Times*
MARCH 9, 1997

*T*he main thing is that I understand the emotional side. It's science and art. With Oprah and me, it was the emotional issues of why and when she ate.

—Bob Greene, personal trainer,
quoted in the *St. Paul Pioneer
Press* (Minnesota)
OCTOBER 21, 1996

*S*he can look at food and put on weight.

—Bob Greene, personal trainer,
quoted in the *Chicago Tribune*
SEPTEMBER 12, 1996

I would take a bullet for her.

—Producer Mary Kay Clinton, as
reported in the *New York Times*
APRIL 14, 1996

*O*prah did the literary
equivalent of inventing penicillin.
Honestly, how many people
would have read so many
of these wonderful books
without her?

—Pat Eisemann, Scribner vice
president and director of publicity,
quoted in *Entertainment Weekly*
APRIL 19, 2002

*W*e couldn't think of anybody more credible than Oprah Winfrey.

—Mary Kubitskey, advertising
manager for Pontiac, in the
Wichita Eagle
SEPTEMBER 18, 2004

*I*f it's on Oprah's list, it will jump right on the best-sellers' list.

—Jay McElroy, a Wal-Mart store
manager, quoted in *Gazette*
(Colorado Springs)
June 21, 2003

I think it's fantastic that she is promoting books and generating interest in quality reading.

—Keith Allen, principal librarian in collection services for the Hillsborough County system, quoted in the *Tampa Tribune* (Florida)
MAY 5, 1997

*M*artha [Stewart] is about what you can have, and Oprah is about who you can be, and there is the difference.

—Michelle Goldsmith, a Portland interior and garden designer, quoted in the *Sunday Oregonian*
JUNE 15, 2003

*I*t is virtually impossible to find even a single image or article from the plaintiff's magazine that would not be jarringly out of place in *O, The Oprah Magazine,* and vice versa.

—Judge John G. Koeltl, who threw
out trade infringement accusations
brought by Ronald Brockmeyer,
German publisher of sexually oriented
O Magazine, saying there was no
evidence of any actual confusion
between the publications; cited by
the Associated Press
MARCH 10, 2003

$\mathcal{S}$he obviously feels good about
herself. She used to dress like
her living-room drapes. Now
she's got style and sophistication.

—*Another World*'s
Linda Dano in *People*
SEPTEMBER 18, 1995

I tell them that the woman you have grown to love, the woman you see on television every day, who gets excited about life, who loves to discover and share—that's the same woman I would see every day in the hallway when I worked for her at Harpo, and it's the same woman I partner with on *Dr. Phil.* Success has not changed her.

> —Terry Wood, executive vice president of programming for Paramount Domestic TV, Harpo's partner in producing *Dr. Phil,* quoted in *Television Week*
> APRIL 19, 2004

*S*he has something about her. Number one, she does something that most people don't have a clue of how to do—she knows how to listen. And she really can listen. And she listens not with just her head, she listens with her heart and soul.

—Quincy Jones, musician, music and film producer, and Oprah's friend, on *Good Morning America*
JANUARY 29, 2004